# Challenging the
# Barbie Doll Syndrome:
## A Group Design for
## Working with Adolescent Girls

by
Heather H. Barto
Sarah J. Salkeld

ISBN 1-930572-12-3

Library of Congress Catalog No. 2001087955

Printing (Last Digit)

9   8   7   6   5   4   3   2   1

*Production editor—*

**Don L. Sorenson, Ph.D.**

*Graphic Design—*

**Earl Sorenson**

*Published by—*

**Educational Media Corporation®**
PO Box 21311
Minneapolis, MN 55421-0311

(763) 781-0088

www.**educationalmedia**.com

# Acknowledgments

We would like to thank all the adolescent girls we have worked with for your candidness and openness about insecurities regarding body image. Thank you for allowing us into your world and sharing your pain and insights with us.

We would like to thank all of our mentors and colleagues who have provided us with such wonderful support and patience, encouragement and knowledge. Above all else, thank you for making us believe that school counselors really do make a difference each and every day. We would like to especially thank:

- **Fred Hanna** for giving us the opportunity for independent study and providing the feedback to make it worthwhile. Your stories and teachings have inspired us and shown us what a truly gifted counselor looks like in action.

- **Rowland Savage** for your enthusiastic support and leadership. Your counseling knowledge, experienced guidance and gentle wisdom has been helpful at so many times and in so many ways.

- **Lynne Muller** for your helpful advice and counseling expertise. We value the constructive feedback you have shared with us about group processing and group dynamics.

We could not possibly forget our families for believing in us and our dreams. Thank you for never asking why or what if, instead simply supporting our idea, which is now a reality. We deeply appreciate your endless love, help and support as we weathered the ups and downs of this adventure together.

## About the Authors

**Heather Heinfelden Barto** graduated with a BS in Psychology from James Madison University in Virginia. She continued her education at Johns Hopkins University, where she graduated with her Master's degree in School Guidance and Counseling. She then completed an Advanced Certificate Program in Counseling At-Risk Adolescents at Johns Hopkins. She has worked in the Baltimore County Public School System at an alternative high school for students who have been expelled from their regular high school and at a high-risk middle school. She is currently on temporary leave from the school system to devote more time to her newly expanded family.

**Sarah Judson Salkeld** graduated with a BS in Psychology from Juniata College in Pennsylvania. She then completed a Masters in School Counseling and an Advanced Certificate in Counseling At-Risk Adolescents from Johns Hopkins University. She has worked primarily with high-risk middle school and high school students. Prior to entering the field of school counseling, she worked as a vocational counselor for individuals with disabilities. This is her first published work.

# Table of Contents

# The Barbie Doll Syndrome

In recent years, psychological research has examined the negative impact of the media on self image. It is commonly accepted that the way in which beauty is defined by our culture through the mass media negatively impacts the development of a healthy self concept. This is especially true for adolescent females as they struggle to become comfortable in their changing bodies. As adolescent girls attempt to incorporate cultural ideals of beauty into their definition of self, they often are confronted with what is sometimes referred to as the Barbie Doll Syndrome. As part of this phenomena, adolescents girls strive to conform to ideals that are not only unrealistic, but dangerously unhealthy.

Heather H. Barto and Sarah J. Salkeld

# Welcome

We would like to take a moment to tell you who we are and why we wrote this book. We met at a middle school just outside of Baltimore, Maryland. As we got to know each other, we learned that we both graduated with our master's degrees in counseling from Johns Hopkins University. At the same time, we completed a post-master's certificate program in counseling at-risk youth—also at Johns Hopkins University. We have had the opportunity to work together in a high-risk middle school for several years, developing an excellent working relationship and a lasting friendship.

While we were on maternity leave with our beautiful girls, Chloe and Madison, we got this great idea. Over the years, both of us ran many groups, but each time we felt that in order to meet the needs of our students effectively, we needed to develop our own group curriculum. For the most part, the group designs that we found were too general and really boring. Thinking that maybe other counselors were experiencing the same frustrations, we decided to write down our group curriculum for working with adolescent girls. It concerned us that adolescent girls were trying to attain the impossible standards of beauty set forth by such a ridiculous thing as a child's toy, like the Barbie doll, and were losing themselves in the process. The curriculum we developed covers such topics as body image, eating disorders, and self-concept. It is our hope that you will find it an excellent resource and use it often. We do.

This book was written specifically for professional school counselors, but counselors in others settings can also use it. If you are such a professional, just ignore all of the school jargon and adapt it to fit your needs.

Finally, we would like to thank you for purchasing this book. We hope you find it helpful. If you like it, please tell other counselors about it.

*Heather Barto    Sarah Salkeld*

# How to Use This Book

We hope you will find this book easy to understand and use. We have tried to design it that way. Before you get started, we would like to call your attention to a few things.

The first part of this book provides information on group process and dynamics, working with adolescent girls, and eating disorders. This information should be helpful to refresh and refocus before you begin. We know that most of you probably won't read it, but it is there for you if you need it. The information on eating disorders is for you to use, but it also can be used as a handout for group members, parents, or teachers. We strongly encourage you to read this section before beginning the sessions on eating disorders, so that the information is fresh in your mind.

The second part of this book provides the lesson plans for the group sessions. To make them easy to implement, they are all presented in the following format:

**Materials:** Make sure you have the required materials ready before your group begins.

**Getting Started:** Each group session should open with fishbowl questions—an icebreaker designed to get your group settled and focused. If you are short on time, you may leave this step out. But, if possible, try to include a shortened version, such as giving only one question to the group.

**Activity:** This step provides the fuel for the discussion that is to follow. Watch your time on this section. Be sure you allow time for discussion.

**Processing:** By far, this is the most important part of the lesson. Challenge your group to look at themselves and to share at this time.

**Journal:** Make sure you give time for this. It is important that each group member has time to reflect individually. Collect the journals at the end of each session so that they can be returned at the last session.

**Closing:** A quick activity to bring closure to the session. Do an informal evaluation of your group at this point and make sure that each member is ready to leave. You may need to let one or two stay behind, if the session was especially powerful.

Don't forget to allow yourself a few minutes after the group is over to meet with group members (if needed) or to compose yourself. Leading a group of this nature can be very draining, so allow yourself a few minutes to sit back, relax, and think objectively about the group session.

# Chapter 1

# Group Dynamics

# Group Counseling

Counselors in the school system are bombarded with demands from every direction. Parents request guidance in dealing with their rebellious children. School administrators seek you out for creative alternatives to suspension and behavior management.

Most importantly, the students need you as an objective listener in a world where they often feel they are not heard. Because of this, counselors often find themselves in a mode that is more reactive than proactive.

Group counseling provides counselors with an avenue to reach several students with similar needs at one time. Additionally, groups provide a format that can proactively address the needs of students.

The group process is a difficult one, especially when working with the adolescent age group. Adolescence is a time of searching for identity and developing a sense of self. As adolescents trudge through this process, they often feel a sense of loneliness about their experiences and develop self-absorbed perceptions. They are torn between wanting to be independent and needing a sense of security to anchor themselves. Adolescents rebel against limits and constantly test boundaries, yet they find the experience of freedom frightening.

The group process allows adolescents the opportunity to verbalize and discuss their feelings. Additionally, it provides a safe environment to experiment with self-expression, develop a stronger sense of self-understanding, and redefine relationships with others.

# Setting Up the Counseling Group

Before getting started with a group, it is necessary to get the word out to students and staff. They need to be informed about the general purpose of the group, so that they may refer students and students can self-refer. After a list has been generated of possible group candidates, you must screen the students. This step often is viewed as unnecessary or too time consuming; however, it is vital. If candidates are not screened, there is a high likelihood that some students will be inappropriate for this type of group. When students are screened, you first want to explain why you called them down to your office. It is necessary to explain what a small counseling group is like and how groups can sometimes help people. You then want to screen with questions such as:

- Why do you think your teachers thought you would be a good match for this group?
- How would your teachers describe you?
- How do you think involvement in a group would help you?
- Tell me about a time when you felt your life was great.
- Tell me about a time when you felt really good about yourself.
- Do you have any questions about the group?

Make sure to emphasize that involvement in a counseling group is voluntary and confidential. Students need to understand that they have control as to whether or not they choose to participate. You are looking for students that verbalize feelings of not liking themselves, view their weight as problematic, have made comments about extreme dieting, or believe that they are not accepted.

Once you have selected the participants for your group, it is important to stress that they have made a commitment. They have decided to become involved. The group process will be beneficial only if they remain involved and committed. For example, showing up for group because it is better than going to class, or showing up but not actively participating, makes group a waste of time. You need to put responsibility on the students by stressing the fact that they will only get out of group what they put into it. Explain to your group members that, at times, topics will be addressed that may be difficult or uncomfortable to talk about, but that this is how personal growth occurs.

# Getting Started and the First Session

As you begin your group, rules must be discussed. The purpose of rules is to ensure that a safe, nonthreatening environment has been created. Rules provide a safety net for risk taking and allow some definition to the time spent together as a group.

Rules should encompass three major concepts: respect, confidentiality, and voluntary participation. These basic concepts can be stated many ways, but all need to be addressed. If your group members do not feel that they are respected or information that is shared will remain confidential, the overall dynamic of your group is weak. When working with adolescents, it is also important to spend some time discussing the fact that group is a time to listen and share. It needs to be stressed that all group members will be given the opportunity to share, but each group member can choose whether or not to share when it is her turn.

As the group begins, expect it to take a few sessions for your group members to reach a level of personal comfort. Sharing can be extremely scary for adolescents, and many will not fully engage in the group process until they feel safe. Developing trust in the group process and in the other group members is a gradual process. As a group facilitator, this is a time to simply be affirming toward each member and to help your group members feel comfortable with each other. Validation of feelings and nonjudgement of statements is extremely important in the beginning sessions.

# Group Dynamics

As the sessions progress, it will become apparent that trust has been established, as group members begin to share more personal details of their lives. Conversations will shift from discussion about favorite movies to feelings about family and friends. The sessions are designed with this in mind; in that, the initial activities are very nonthreatening. However, the session activities and questions gradually focus more on the individual self. During this time, it is important to emphasize the discussion part of the session outline. Irrational statements and negative self-perceptions should be challenged and discussed. You should use questioning techniques that allow your group members to really think about their individual feelings and perceptions. This is the point where the group process can really foster growth and change.

The final sessions are a time of closure and reflection. Your group members need to be encouraged to reflect on previous sessions and to discuss what was learned. At this point, your group has developed a bond, and group members need to be given the opportunity to discuss their feelings relating to ending the time spent together. It is a positive sign for group members to express a desire for this group to continue. You can address this by discussing ways that the group members can reinforce what was learned about self, such as continued writing in their journals or the use of self-affirmations.

# Common Problems/Practical Solutions

### The Non-Stop Talker:

Adolescents often love the experience of sharing and having attention focused on themselves. Because of this, some individual group members may tend to dominate the process. If this happens, it needs to be addressed immediately. This can be done through a group discussion: ("Sue, you have shared a lot today about your experiences. I am wondering what the other group members are thinking about?") Or, through an individual session: ("Sue, I have noticed you tend to talk a lot in group. I am pleased you are so comfortable sharing with the group; however, sometimes there is not enough time for the other group members to talk. Perhaps next session, you could try to focus on helping the other group members share more.")

### The Quiet Observer:

For some adolescents, the group experience is new and possibly intimidating. Some group members will naturally feel more comfortable sharing and others will need some encouragement to actively participate. Our group sessions are designed to provide opportunities for structured participation, where all group members are given the opportunity to respond and share. However, if certain group member(s) only participate when prompted or appear hesitant to disclose, this should be addressed. Nonparticipation can sometimes indicate discomfort with the group process, which is counterproductive to personal growth. This issue can be addressed individually: ("Sue, I have noticed that you are pretty quiet in group. I am wondering how you feel the group is going? How do you think group is helping you?") Sometimes it is also helpful to address it in the group format, through establishing connections among the group members: ("Sue, I wonder if you feel the same as Amy about....")

## Off-Task Behavior:

When working with adolescents, you will discover almost immediately that they are masters at changing the subject. Often when the session involves personal disclosure or self-analysis, it becomes easier for the group members to lighten the conversation by bringing up irrelevant information. Sometimes, a group member will start talking about a music group or an unfair teacher. At times, a group member may utilize humor (acting silly or sharing a joke) to channel the focus to something less threatening. Some of these tactics represent normal adolescent behavior; however, if allowed to continue, these behaviors will seriously hinder the growth of the group. As the group leader, this can be addressed as an observation: ("I am noticing a lot of silliness/giggling today and wonder what is going on? Is it possible that what we are talking about today is making you feel a little uncomfortable?" I wonder why it is so much easier to talk about music than it is to talk about our feelings?")

## Parental Concerns:

In some situations, parents may contact the school requesting information about your group. Sharing generic information about your group is always a good approach. For example: ("The counseling department facilitates a variety of groups for our students to help with problem-solving and decision-making skills.") At times, you may receive phone calls from parents demanding to know what is being discussed within the group. This is usually a reaction to something their child has shared with them and should be explored from that perspective: ("Mrs. Smith, it seems like you have some concerns about the group. What are your concerns?") If you respond by stating that group discussions are confidential and information can not be shared, an automatic barrier to communication will be created. Rather, without betraying confidentiality, it is important to communicate openly with the parent about concerns. If the parent wants to know specifically what his or her child has been discussing in your group, the most effective approach is to reiterate the purpose of the group: ("Your daughter participates in this group on a weekly basis to help her develop a more positive view about herself.")

# Chapter 2

# Working with Adolescent Girls

# Working with Adolescent Girls

*"Something dramatic happens to girls in early adolescence. Just as planes and ships disappear over the Bermuda Triangle, so do the selves of girls go down in droves. They crash and burn in a social and developmental Bermuda Triangle.... They lose their resiliency and optimism and become less curious and inclined to take risks. They lose their assertive energetic and "tomboyish" personalities and become more deferential, self-critical, and depressed. They report great unhappiness with their bodies."*

Mary Pipher author of

*Reviving Ophelia*

As adolescent girls struggle to develop their own identity, they are constantly bombarded with messages about what their identity should be. The media defines what beauty looks like, how thin a female body should be, what clothing will make one more popular, and even what scents will make one more desirable. These messages are extremely powerful and generate cultural expectations for girls which are often confusing and convoluted. For example, girls should be beautiful, but looks aren't everything. Girls should be sexy, but not sexual. Girls should be honest, but not hurt anyone's feelings. Girls should be independent, but nice. Girls should try hard, but not be competitive. Girls should be smart, but not so smart that they threaten boys.

For the adolescent girl, these messages about what girls should be overpower how they have defined themselves in preadolescent years. According to Pipher, with the onset of puberty, girls feel enormous cultural pressure to develop a false self, which is an identity defined by others rather than self. This cultural pressure not only comes from the media, but from parents, peers, and the opposite sex. "Girls believe that they can be true to themselves and risk abandonment by their peers, or they can reject their true selves and be socially acceptable."

As the adolescent girl fluctuates between what she wants to be and what she thinks she is supposed to be, many visible changes can be observed. Behavior is erratic and unpredictable. What she likes one day, she detests the next day. Thought patterns are characterized by black and white concreteness. School is either wonderful or pure torture. Friends are either fantastic or mean. Minor events, such as a reprimand from a teacher or a negative comment about clothing, seem catastrophic and often result in extreme emotional reactions. Emotions are chaotic and intense, with wild fluctuations in mood. She can be okay one minute and in tears the next.

Heather H. Barto and Sarah J. Salkeld

Developmentally, changes are also occurring with the physical self, which often leads to an intense preoccupation with outward appearances. Perceptions about body size become increasingly negative and hypercritical. Suddenly, thighs are perceived as fat, the stomach is viewed as flabby, and breasts are either too big or too small. Girls begin to be affected by societal ideals of thinness and beauty, leading to the belief that their bodies are imperfect. Slowly, self-concept is defined by the cultural ideal, which often generates a futile and self-destructive search to create a perfect body.

In the classroom, changes can be observed, both in the way girls are perceived and in their academic performance. Research on classroom behaviors indicates that boys are five times more likely to receive attention from the teacher and twelve times more likely to speak up in class. Additionally, boys are more likely to be praised for academic and intellectual ability, whereas girls are more likely to be praised for behaving properly and obeying the rules. American Association of University Women (AAUW) studies repeatedly show that there is a dramatic shift in the academic achievement of girls during this time. For example, in elementary school, girls outperform boys on standard measures of achievement and adjustment, but by high school, they are behind boys. Furthermore, girls know that math is important, but often view it as masculine and something they are not good at. Pipher believes that diminished success in math is due to the fact that math requires exactly the same qualities that adolescent girls lack: "confidence, trust in one's judgment and the ability to tolerate frustration." It seems that girls are socialized to value achievement, only to the point that it doesn't interfere with social popularity and femininity.

# Why a Group on this Topic?

As girls enter adolescence, they are at-risk. The intense preoccupation with the physical self, combined with emotional insecurity, make this a time of increased risk for eating disorders. The victims of eating disorders are often the high achievers and the ones that appear most well adjusted. As girls begin to incorporate cultural values of beauty and perfection, they are at-risk for developing an unhealthy self-concept. Adolescent girls need to be encouraged and shown how to develop identities based on talents and interests, rather than appearance, sexuality, or popularity.

According to C. Gilligan and K. Johnson, adolescent girls need to develop the following skills in order to have a healthy concept of self. This information can be formatted into group goals when working with adolescent girls.

- Ability to confront fears about displeasing others
- Ability to express feelings to others honestly
- Establishment of friendships only with people who respect her and her feelings
- Knowledge of likes, wants, and needs and willingness to ask for it
- Ability to recognize shortcomings, accept them, and take criticism without it impacting feelings of self-worth
- Ability to take credit for accomplishments/talents
- Ability to be comfortable making positive statements about herself to others
- Identification of goals/dreams for the future

It is our belief that any group format that provides an opportunity for discussion about self-image and teaches habits for coping with stress will be beneficial to adolescent girls. As adolescent girls often know much more about other's feelings than their own, they need the opportunity to explore individual feelings and to focus on self-nurturing. The group that we have developed facilitates an avenue for open discussion by gently challenging societal values and teaching strategies for maintaining a healthy identity. It is our hope that it can help provide a secure foundation for ongoing development.

# Chapter 3

# Information on Eating Disorders

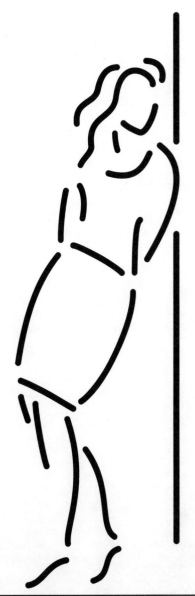

# Important Information on Eating Disorders

This section of the manual is designed to give you some quick fact and information sheets about eating disorders. You may use this information to refresh yourself on the particulars of eating disorders or use them as handouts for parents, teachers, administrators, and students.

Much of the information provided in the next several pages is adapted from ANRED (Anorexia Nervosa and Related Eating Disorders, Inc.). ANRED is a nonprofit organization staffed by medical and counseling professionals that provides information about a variety of eating disorders. If you are interested in learning more about them, or contacting them with questions, you can reach them by phone at 1-800-931-2237 or through their website at www.anred.com. You can pose questions to them through the website and they will provide excellent responses in a prompt manner.

Please remember that the information provided is not a substitute for medical advice or treatment. For help with the physical and/or medical problems associated with eating disorders, please refer to a physician.

# Anorexia Nervosa

## Physical Signs:

- Significant weight loss, often in a short period of time
- Weighs less than 85% of what is expected for age and height
- Refusal to maintain normal body weight for age and height
- Amenorrhea (absence of menstrual period)
- Intolerance to cold
- Dizziness and fainting
- Dry skin
- Loss of muscle
- Impaired concentration

## Behavioral Signs:

- Restricted food intake
- Unusual food rituals or strange eating habits (Examples: Counting food bites, cutting food into tiny pieces, moving food around on plate without eating)
- Intense fear of becoming fat, even when dangerously thin
- Dressing in layers or baggy clothes
- Binge-eating (50% of anorexics have bulimic tendencies)
- Regular weighing
- Denies dangers associated with low weight

## Attitudinal Signs:

- Severe mood changes
- Perfectionist standards resulting in feeling of insecurity
- Need to be withdrawn or isolated
- Dichotomous thinking (Example: viewing food in extreme divisions of good/safe and bad/dangerous)
- Distorted body image

# Bulimia Nervosa

### Physical Signs:

- Frequent weight fluctuations
- Swollen salivary glands, puffiness in cheeks, and/or broken blood vessels under the eye
- Light headedness of dizziness
- Tooth decay and receding gums

### Behavioral Signs:

- Binge eating and secretive eating
- Diets when not binge eating
- Purging, vomiting, laxative abuse, diuretics, enema, and/or intense exercise
- May shoplift, be promiscuous, or abuse drugs or alcohol
- Preoccupation with food and weight
- Avoidance of social events involving food
- Bathroom visits following meals
- Intense fear of being fat, in spite of normal or near normal weight
- Taking care of other people's needs before own

### Attitudinal Signs:

- Frequent mood changes
- Feelings of depression, sadness, shame, guilt, and/ or loneliness
- Severe self-criticism
- Need for approval from others
- Self-worth determined by weight
- Feels unworthy
- Has difficulty talking about feelings

# Medical Complications of Eating Disorders

If not stopped, starving or binge eating and purging cycles can lead to irreversible physical damage to the body or even death. Eating disorders affect every cell, tissue, and organ in the human body. The following is a partial list of the medical dangers associated with anorexia and bulimia.

- Irregular heart beat and/or cardiac arrest
- Kidney damage
- Liver damage
- Destruction or decay of teeth
- Damage or rupture to the esophagus
- Loss of muscle mass
- Disruption of menstrual cycle and fertility problems
- Weakened immune system
- Swollen glands in neck or face
- Excessive hair on face or body
- Dry skin
- Malnutrition
- Fainting spells
- Sleep disruptions
- Mental fuzziness
- Loss of bone mass

**Important:** Eating disorders are treatable and people *do* recover from them. The above list of complications or the threat of them developing should encourage people to seek treatment and not give up. Sooner is better than later. The sooner medical treatment begins, the less the damage is done to the body and the more able medical professionals are to help the person to become physically healthy.

# Psychological Concerns Associated with Eating Disorders

It is ironic that a person who develops an eating disorder often begins with a diet, thinking that weight loss will lead to improved self-confidence and higher self-esteem. The reality is that persistent undereating, binge eating, and purging cycles have the opposite effect. Individuals with eating disorders tend to struggle with one or more of the following psychological complications:

- Depression, which can lead to suicide
- Feeling out of control or helpless
- Anxiety
- Self-doubt
- Guilt and/or shame
- Terrified of discovery
- Obsessive thoughts or preoccupation about weight and food
- Compulsive behaviors
- Ritualistic behavior
- Feelings of alienation and loneliness
- Feelings of hopelessness
- Suicidal ideations

**Important:** Eating disorders are treatable and people *do* recover from them. The above list of concerns or the threat of them developing should encourage people to seek treatment and not give up. Sooner is better than later. The sooner treatment begins, the sooner the person can achieve personal strength and create a life worth living.

Heather H. Barto and Sarah J. Salkeld

# Eating Disorders and Recovery

Eating disorders are treatable and people do recover from them. Recovery is a difficult process that can take several months, or even years. Some people do better than others. People who do the best, work with doctors and counselors who help them to resolve medical and psychological issues associated with disordered eating.

Recovery is much more than stopping the starving or binge eating and purging cycles. At the very least it involves the following:

- Maintenance of normal or near normal weight
- Regular menstrual periods
- A varied diet of normal foods
- Elimination of or major reduction in irrational fears about food
- Age appropriate relationships with friends and family
- Strong problem-solving skills
- Fun activities that have nothing to do with food and/or weight
- Understanding about making decisions and consequences
- Realistic sense of self and goals for the future

The average time it takes someone suffering from an eating disorder to recover is five years. That means that the person is maintaining a healthy weight and eating a balanced diet with a variety of normal foods. This person also participates in meaningful relationships with friends and family. She is working hard in school or at a career. Most say that they feel stronger and more insightful about themselves and life in general.

# Eating Disorders and Treatment

Treatment can take many forms. In order to determine the best treatment for an individual, an evaluation with a doctor and/or a counselor is needed. Several treatment options are listed below with the rational for each.

- **Hospitalization** to prevent death, suicide, or medical crisis
- **Medication** to help manage anxiety or depression
- **Dental work** to repair damage and prevent future problems
- **Individual counseling** to develop healthy ways of taking control of life
- **Group counseling** to learn how to build healthy relationships
- **Family counseling** to change patterns of behavior within the family unit and create new healthy ones
- **Nutritional counseling** to examine food myths and design balanced meals and encourage healthy eating habits
- **Support groups** to break down isolation and share with others who have similar experiences

Finding help with treatment options may be easier than you think.

If it is a crisis situation, call a crisis hotline which can be found in your local yellow pages, call 911, or go to a hospital emergency room.

If it is not a crisis, contact your doctor and ask for an evaluation and a referral to the appropriate treatment option. Do not feel embarrassed about sharing this information with your doctor; doctors are trained to deal with this kind of situation.

You may also check with a counselor in the area or in a school for help or more information about treatment options.

# Eating Disorder Statistics

- Studies indicate that over half of women and adolescent females list appearance among the biggest concerns of their lives.

- Research suggests that approximately 1% of female adolescents have anorexia. In other words, one out of every one hundred women between the ages of ten and twenty are starving themselves, sometimes to death.

- Research suggests that 4% of females in college suffer from bulimia. In other words, four out of every hundred women in college are binge eating and then compensating by doing things like throwing up or abusing laxatives.

- Without treatment, 20% of people with serious eating disorders die. With treatment that number drops to less than 3%.

- With treatment, 60% of people with eating disorders recover. They maintain a healthy weight and eat a balanced diet of normal foods. They develop meaningful relationships and have careers.

- About 20% of people with eating disorders who seek treatment make a partial recovery. They continue to stay extremely focused on food and weight. They seldom have meaningful friendships, and tend to have jobs rather than careers.

- The remaining 20% do not improve even with treatment. Their lives continue to revolve around food and weight and they very likely will become depressed, lonely, and hopeless. They are often frequent patients in eating disorder treatment programs and even emergency rooms.

- Unfortunately, since the study of eating disorders is relatively new, there is not a great deal of information on the long-term recovery process. However, we do know that on average recovery from an eating disorder takes about five years.

- Because eating disorders are often secretive in nature, it is very difficult to determine the exact number of people who suffer from them.

# Warning Signs of Eating Disorders

- Preoccupation with weight, food, or appearance
- Making excuses as to why she is not eating during meals
- Dissatisfied with weight, in spite of excessive weight loss
- Going to bathroom frequently after meals
- Smell of vomit in bathroom
- Excessive exercise
- Always cold
- Wearing layers of clothing to hide weight loss
- Strange food behaviors
- Loss of thinning of hair
- Frequent weighing
- Buying large amounts of food that disappear quickly
- Isolating self from friends and family
- Onset of severe tooth decay
- Collecting recipes
- Wants to bake for friends and family, but does not eat with them
- Use of laxatives, diuretics, and/or diet pills
- Depressive moods
- Frequent overeating, especially when upset or stressed

# Suggestions for Friends and Family

The biggest problem is most likely convincing the person to get help. At first, she will probably deny there is a problem and resist help. She may not want to try to change. It may be a while before a person with an eating disorder is ready to seek help. In the meantime, here are some things to keep in mind as you try to help.

## Things to do:

- Be respectful.
- Realize that the person will not change until she is ready.
- Provide information.
- Be supportive and caring.
- Be a good listener.
- Continue to suggest professional help.
- Talk about the advantages of recovery and living a healthy life.
- Agree that recovery is hard, but very possible.
- Offer to go with her to the counselor or doctor the first time.
- Realize that recovery is her responsibility.

## Things to avoid:

- Don't nag, beg, bribe, or threaten.
- Avoid power struggles.
- Never criticize.
- Do not use shame or guilt.
- Don't try to control.
- Don't give advice, unless you are asked.
- Don't say things like "You're too thin."
- Don't ignore stolen food or evidence of purging. Ask for responsibility.
- Don't underestimate what you can accomplish.

Heather H. Barto and Sarah J. Salkeld

# Chapter 4

# Group Design

## Session 1:
# Introduction

**Goal:**

By participating in the introductory activities, group members will become acquainted with other group members and the group process.

**Materials:**

*Self-Esteem Survey: How Do You Feel About Yourself?* (page 34)

*How Do We Measure Up?* (page 35)

Session 1: Fishbowl Questions

Journals for Group Members (group members can be asked to provide)

**Getting Started:**

Group members will independently complete the *Self-Esteem Survey* which will serve as a pre-test. Give the same survey to them at the conclusion of the twelve group sessions to evaluate progress.

Group members will introduce themselves by sharing their names and choosing a question from the fishbowl. Each person will read a question aloud and share her response with the group.

Discuss the rules for the group.

It is important to stress that if there are too many rules, nobody will remember them; therefore, the rules will have no significance. Allow your group members the opportunity to suggest rules. You may find that they are suggesting rules that are appropriate for a classroom, but are not pertinent in a small group setting, such as: raising hands, gum chewing, and so forth. If this occurs, you may need to provide some clarification about the difference between classroom learning and small group counseling. Some rules that definitely need to be considered are the following:

**Confidentiality, Right to Pass, Respect for All.** The following more clearly defines these primary rules:

**Confidentiality:** Everything that is shared in the group is private and should not be repeated outside the group setting.

**Right to Pass:** Participation in the group is important, but no one will ever be forced to share if it is uncomfortable to do so.

**Respect for All:** This rule covers a broad spectrum of appropriate group behavior, (i.e, no interruptions, no name calling, and no laughing at the expense of another group member). Several rules suggested by group members usually can be combined to fall under this rule.

**Activity:**  Group members will participate in the *How Do We Measure Up?* activity as a group. This activity is designed to be an icebreaker and to foster group cohesiveness. The group as a whole should complete the activity. Instruct them to take turns reading a question and recording the appropriate responses from each group member. Each group member should be responsible for at least one question.

**Journal:**  At the end of each session, give your group a writing prompt as part of a reflective writing activity. Provide the writing prompt (a question or a sentence stem) and then allow approximately five minutes of quiet time for them to self reflect and write. For this part of the session, a notebook needs to be provided to each. It is usually helpful for you to keep your students' folders/journals between group meetings. Encourage them to share parts of their journal entries at the end of group sessions. However, journals are confidential; group members should never by required to share entries if they are not comfortable doing so.

For the first session, instruct them to complete the following sentence in their journals:

> Something I learned today....

Encourage them to write thoughts and feelings they experienced in the group today.

**Closing:**  Ask your group to share a sentence or two from their journal entries. It should be a quick thought or feeling statement that sums up their reactions to the group today. They should not read their entire journal entry, just share one small thought or feeling from it.

# Self-Esteem Survey:
# How Do You Feel About Yourself?

Name:_____

On a scale of 1-5, circle the number that best describes how you feel about yourself.

    1 = very untrue; 5 = very true

| | | | | | |
|---|---|---|---|---|---|
| I feel good about the way I look. | 1 | 2 | 3 | 4 | 5 |
| I like the way I dress. | 1 | 2 | 3 | 4 | 5 |
| I feel good about my grades. | 1 | 2 | 3 | 4 | 5 |
| I think my parents are proud of me. | 1 | 2 | 3 | 4 | 5 |
| I feel good about the friends I have. | 1 | 2 | 3 | 4 | 5 |
| I like my personality. | 1 | 2 | 3 | 4 | 5 |
| I feel comfortable around my friends. | 1 | 2 | 3 | 4 | 5 |
| I feel comfortable around boys. | 1 | 2 | 3 | 4 | 5 |
| My friends accept me for who I am. | 1 | 2 | 3 | 4 | 5 |
| I have a positive attitude about myself. | 1 | 2 | 3 | 4 | 5 |
| I like most things about myself. | 1 | 2 | 3 | 4 | 5 |
| People like me. | 1 | 2 | 3 | 4 | 5 |

        Heather H. Barto and Sarah J. Salkeld

# How Do We Measure Up?

Each group member will take a turn. When it is your turn, read a question out loud and ask each group member to share her information to help complete the question. The idea is to get as many points as possible.

_____ 1. Total the number of sisters each group member has in her family.

_____ 2. Total the number of pets each group member has in her home.

_____ 3. Total the number of musical instruments that group members can play.

_____ 4. Total the number of hair accessories in group members' hair.

_____ 5. Total all the shoe sizes of the group members.

_____ 6. Total the number of different states group members have lived in.

_____ 7. Total the number of television shows each group member watches per night.

_____ 8. Total the number of letters in each group member's middle name.

## Session 1: Fishbowl Questions

**What if clothing was free?**

**What if cats could get a driver's license?**

**What if the principal of the school was a ten-year-old girl?**

**What if parents couldn't talk?**

**What if you had to be 25 years old to eat ice cream?**

**What if all people looked exactly alike?**

**What if chocolate grew on trees?**

**What if there were no traffic lights?**

**What if school did not exist?**

**What if wearing jeans was illegal?**

# Session 2:
# Group Collage—"The Perfect Female"

**Goals:**

Group members will explore the concept of self-esteem in order to increase awareness of distorted perceptions by creating a collage representing the "perfect female."

Group members will learn more about other group members in order to increase group cohesion by engaging in guided casual conversation.

**Note:** Session 3 builds on this session.

**Materials:**

Session 2: Fishbowl Questions

Glue

Scissors

Magazines

Journal Entry and Journals

**Getting Started:**

A group member will select a question from the fishbowl and respond to her question. There will be time for one or two brief comments from the group. The next group member will then select a question and respond. The process will repeat itself until each group member has been given the opportunity to respond to a question.

**Activity:**

Group members will work to create a collage depicting the "perfect female." They should be encouraged to talk and get to know each other through casual conversation. (See Processing Section.)

**Processing:**

This collage activity will be fully processed in the next session. The purpose of this session is to allow the group members time to work on their collages while learning more about each other and sharing about themselves. You should permit the conversation to be casual in nature, while providing some guidance. You can facilitate this conversation by asking questions such as:

- What are your interests?
- What do you do with your time outside of school?
- What is your favorite thing to do on the weekends?
- Describe your family.

It is important to point out similarities and to connect/include individuals by saying thing like:

- So Mary and Susan, you both play soccer....
- Has anyone else experienced that?
- Who haven't we heard from yet?
- Does anyone have anything to add to that thought?
- Is anyone else interested in that movie or TV show?
- It seems that both Judy and Daphne have large families....

**Caution:** Make sure they do not become so involved in the discussion that they do not finish the collage. It is important that they focus on the activity, as well as participate in the conversation. If they do not complete the activity, it will be difficult to process it in next session.

**Journal:** Take the last few minutes of the session to have them respond in their journals to the following writing prompt:

> Describe the "perfect female."

**Closing:** Ask them to share a sentence or two from their journal entries. It should be a quick thought or feeling statement that sums up her reaction to the group today. They should not read their entire journal entry, just share one small thought or feeling from it.

## Session 2: Fishbowl Questions

**What is the best movie you have ever seen?**

**What famous person would you like to meet?**

**If you could be an animal, what would you be and why?**

**What was the best day of your life?**

**What is your earliest memory?**

**What is your favorite color?**

**What is your favorite television show?**

**What is your favorite season and why?**

**If you had $5,000.00 dollars, what would you do with it?**

**What is your favorite music group?**

## Session 3:
# Group Collage—"The Perfect Female"

**Goal:** Group members will explore the concept of self-esteem in order to increase awareness of distorted perceptions by discussing their collages representing the "perfect female" made in the previous session.

**Materials:** Session 3: Fishbowl Questions

"Perfect Female" collage

Journal Entry and Journals

**Getting Started:** A group member will select a question from the fishbowl and respond to her question. There will be time for one or two brief comments from the group. The next group member will then select a question and respond. The process will repeat itself until each group member has been given the opportunity to respond to a question

**Activity:** Give your group members several minutes to look over their collages and their journal entries from the previous session. The remainder of the session (with the exception of the last five minutes, which will be devoted to the journal entry,) will be used to process the collages and perceptions of the perfect female. (See Processing Section.)

**Processing:** This is a very important session to give your group members the chance to look at the misconceptions and inaccurate information they may have received about females. Each person should be given several minutes to describe her collage and explain what each portion represents to her. During this time, it is important to demonstrate active listening skills and to encourage other group members to do the same. If any group members interrupt each other, make sure you gently remind them to stay focused on the speaker and her collage. After each person has explained her collage, stop and allow others to ask questions before moving on to the next collage. If they do not delve deep enough into the thoughts and feeling behind the creation of the collage, make sure you do. It is important to ask questions about the collage's content as well as the ideas behind the pictures. Questions you might want to ask or encourage other group members to ask are:

- What does that picture/figure symbolize/represent to you?
- Why was it important for you to include that?
- Do you think this is an accurate representation of the perfect female?
- Is there anything else you wanted to add but could not find?
- What does that picture mean to you?

- How do you feel about your finished collage?
- Which part has the most meaning for you? Why?
- What were you thinking about when you made the collage?
- What feelings came up as you were making your collage?

It is extremely important that you take your time and fully process each collage. Your group members may get a little silly if the conversation becomes too deep and they become uncomfortable. Reflect this behavior back to them by saying something like: "It seems we are all getting a little off-task. Could that be because what we are talking about is a difficult thing to discuss?" or "I am not sure what is going on here, but it appears we are losing our focus. Does anyone have an idea as to what is happening today?"

This will usually get the desired response. If not, you need to delve a little deeper into the behavior to determine its cause and eliminate it.

**Journal:** Ask your group members to take the last few minutes of the group to respond in their journals to the following writing prompt:

How had your perception of the perfect female changed since the last group meeting?

**Closing:** Individual group members should share a sentence or two from their journal entries. It should be a quick thought or feeling statement that sums up their reactions to the group today. They should not read the entire journal entry—just share one small thought or feeling from it.

## Session 3: Fishbowl Questions

**What is the best movie you have ever seen?**

**What famous person would you like to meet?**

**If you could be an animal, what would you be and why?**

**What was the best day of your life?**

**What is your earliest memory?**

**What is your favorite color?**

**What is your favorite television show?**

**What is your favorite season and why?**

**If you had $5,000.00 dollars, what would you do with it?**

**What is your favorite music group?**

## Session 4:
# Eating Disorders

**Goal:**

Group members will explore the topics of eating disorders, specifically anorexia and bulimia, in order to learn more about eating disorders, examine treatment and prevention strategies, and assess personal risk by viewing a film, participating in a group discussion, reading materials, and completing a personal risk assessment.

**Note:** Session 5 builds on this session.

**Materials:**

Session 4: Fishbowl Questions

Film: *For the Love of Nancy**

Information sheets on Eating Disorders

Journal Entry and Journals

**Getting Started:**

A group member will select a question from the fishbowl and respond to her question. There will be time for one or two brief comments from the group. The next group member will then select a question and respond. The process will repeat itself until each group member has been given the opportunity to respond to a question.

**Activity:**

The group will watch the film, *For the Love of Nancy*. It is best if you can schedule the group over a two-hour period of time so they can watch the movie in one sitting. In the past, we have found that using a lunch period combined with a class period will often provide the time needed. If possible, try to schedule the next session in the same week so that the film is fresh in the group members' minds when they discuss it.

Please refer to the next page for information on obtaining the film, *For the Love of Nancy*. If you are unable to obtain the film, please use the alternate group plan for Session 4.

**Processing:**

This film is an excellent depiction of a woman suffering with anorexia. It will be fully processed in the next session. In the past, we have found it to be excellent for beginning discussions about eating disorders in a non-threatening way. It also provides a clear picture of how quickly a diet can turn into a serious illness.

**Journal:**

Ask your group members to take the last few minutes of the group to respond in their journals to the following writing prompt:

What is your reaction to the film?

**Closing:**	Individual members of your group should share a sentence or two from their journal entries. It should be a quick thought or feeling statement that sums up her reaction to the group today. Group members should not read their entire journal entry—just share one small thought or feeling from it.

### *Note about the movie, *For the Love of Nancy.*

This movie is an excellent portrayal of a teen with an eating disorder and how it affects the entire family system. The authors have found it to be an extremely powerful tool in providing a foundation for discussions on this topic. Unfortunately, the movie is not available on video. However, it is aired monthly on the Lifetime Television Channel. For information on when it will be showing, simply log onto www.lifetimetv.com and type in the title of the movie. The website should then provide you with a schedule of upcoming movie times in the next month. If you do not have internet access, Lifetime Television can be contacted directly at 1-212-424-7000.

## Session 4: Fishbowl Questions

When others put me down, I....

One thing I really dislike about myself is....

I wish my parents knew....

I wear the kind of clothes I do because....

Things would be better in my family if only....

**I secretly wish....**

**The best thing that could happen to my family....**

**I wish my teachers knew....**

**If I could change one thing about myself, I would....**

**One of the hardest things for me is....**

# Session 4:
# Eating Disorders—Alternate Group Plan

**Goal:**

Group members will explore the topics of eating disorders, specifically anorexia and bulimia, in order to learn more about eating disorders, examine treatment and prevention strategies, and assess personal risk by participating in a group discussion, reading materials, and completing a personal risk assessment.

**Note:** If you are using this session then you should skip Session Five and begin again at Session Six.

**Materials:**

Session 4: Fishbowl Questions (Alternate)

Risk Assessment: *Eating Disorders—Are You in Danger?* (see page 54)

Information Sheets on Eating Disorders

Journal Entry and Journals

**Getting Started:**

A group member will select a question from the fishbowl and respond to her question. There will be time for one or two brief comments from the group. The next group member will then select a question and respond. The process will repeat itself until each group member has been given the opportunity to respond to a question.

**Activity:**

Independently, your group members will complete the risk assessment: Eating Disorders—Are You in Danger? Discuss the results with your group. Allow ample time to discuss any questions or concerns that might arise. As the group facilitator, evaluate potential risks by using the following scale:

Number of "yes" responses:

0 - 5   Low Risk

6 - 9   Moderate Risk

10 +   High Risk

**Note:** This scale is not to be shared with your group members. It is for your use as the group facilitator to evaluate risk factors. Please make sure they are accurately interpreting and answering the questions. Look for group members who are responding with a "yes" response to the questions. If she scores in the moderate range, you may want to discuss the assessment with her individually. If she scores in the high range, you need to discuss your findings with her, and most likely, her parents.

It may be necessary to meet with your group members on an individual basis if their responses indicate problem behaviors.

Give your group members the information sheets on eating disorders, which can be found in Chapter 3. Allow time for them to look at the information and proceed with the processing section. If the discussion of the risk assessment takes up the entire discussion time, allow them to take information sheets home.

Heather H. Barto and Sarah J. Salkeld

**Processing:**

In most cases, the risk assessment will provide plenty for your group to discuss. It is important for you, as the group leader, to make sure that your group members have correct information about eating disorders. If they begin to share inaccurate information, be sure to stop and provide correct information. Usually, the group will not need help getting the discussion started. However, if your group is slow to start, you may want to introduce the following questions:

Which questions from the risk assessment do you worry about most?

Do you know someone who might have an eating disorder?

What can you do if you suspect someone has an eating disorder?

**Journal:**

Have your group members take the last few minutes of the group to respond in their journals to the following writing prompt:

What have you learned about eating disorders?

**Closing:**

Group members will be asked to share a sentence or two from their journal entries. It should be a quick thought or feeling statement that sums up her reaction to the group today. Group members should not read the entire journal entry-just share one small thought or feeling from it.

## Session 4: Fishbowl Questions (Alternate)

**One thing I really dislike about myself is....**

**I wish my parents knew....**

**I wear the kind of clothes I do because....**

**Things would be better in my family if only....**

**I secretly wish....**

Heather H. Barto and Sarah J. Salkeld

**The best thing that could happen to my family....**

_____

**I wish my teachers knew....**

_____

**If I could change one thing about myself, I would....**

_____

**One of the hardest things for me is....**

_____

**When other put me down, I....**

_____

# Eating Disorders—Are You in Danger?

The following questionnaire can help you determine if you are at risk for developing an eating disorder. Circle any statements that apply to you.

1. Even though people tell me I am thin, I feel fat.

2. I get anxious if I can't exercise.

3. I worry about what I will eat.

4. If I gain weight, I feel anxious or depressed.

5. I would rather eat by myself than with my friends or family.

6. Other people talk about the way I eat.

7. I get anxious when people urge me to eat.

8. I don't talk about my fear of becoming fat because no one understands how I feel.

9. I enjoy cooking for others, but usually do not eat what I have cooked.

10. I have a secret stash of food.

11. When I eat, I am afraid I will not be able to stop.

12. I lie about what I eat.

13. If I were thinner, I would like myself better.

14. I feel guilty when I eat.

15. I avoid some people because they bug me about what I eat.

16. When I eat, I feel bloated and fat.

17. I get anxious when people watch me eat.

18. I want to be thinner than my friends.

19. I have fasted to lose weight.

20 I am hardly ever satisfied with myself.

*Adapted from ANRED, 2000*

Heather H. Barto and Sarah J. Salkeld

# Session 5:
# Eating Disorders

**Goal:**

Group members will explore the topics of eating disorders, specifically anorexia and bulimia, in order to learn more about eating disorders, examine treatment and prevention strategies, and assess personal risk by viewing a film, participating in a group discussion, reading materials, and completing a personal risk assessment.

**Materials:**

Session 5: Fishbowl Questions

Risk Assessment: *Eating Disorders: Are You in Danger?* (see page 54)

Information Sheets on Eating Disorders

Journal Entry and Journals

**Getting Started:**

A group member will select a question from the fishbowl and respond to her question. There will be time for one or two brief comments from the group. The next group member will then select a question and respond. The process will repeat itself until each group member has been given the opportunity to respond to a question.

**Note:** The Session 5 Fishbowl Questions are the same as those used in Session 4. Make sure that each group member gets a different question from the previous session. If a group member draws the same question selected last week she should choose another question and return the first question to the fishbowl. It is interesting to note that often the responses have changed since the last session.

**Activity:**

Have your group members independently complete the risk assessment *Eating Disorders: Are You in Danger?* Discuss the risk assessment with the group. Allow ample time to discuss any questions or concerns that might arise. As the group facilitator, you will evaluate potential risk by using the following scale:

Number of "yes" responses:

0 - 5   Low Risk

6 - 9   Moderate Risk

10 +   High Risk

**Note:** This scale is not to be shared with group members. It is for your use as the group facilitator to evaluate risk factors. Please make sure your group members are accurately interpreting and answering the questions. Look for those who are responding with "yes" to the questions. If an individual scores in the moderate range, you may want to discuss the assessment with her individually. If a group member scores in the high range, you need to discuss your findings with her, and most likely, her parents.

**Processing:**

The group will process the film, *For the Love of Nancy.* In the past, we have found it to be excellent in beginning discussions about eating disorders in a non-threatening way. It also provides a clear picture of how quickly a diet can turn into a serious illness. As the group talks about the movie, help them to look at the different behaviors and emotions that are shown in the film. You may also want to help them examine the progression of the illness.

The group should not need too much direction because the film is very powerful and discussion is usually easily started. Make sure they stay on topic and are following all of the group rules as they proceed. If the group is slow to start, you may introduce several question to get them started:

How could you tell that Nancy was getting sick?

What kinds of things did she do that seemed strange?

How did her behavior affect the rest of the family?

What were you feeling as you watched the movie?

How did you feel about Nancy?

**Journal:**

Take the last few minutes of the group to have them respond in their journals to the following writing prompt:

What have you learned about eating disorders?

**Closing:**

Give your group the opportunity to gather the information handout that can be found in Chapter 3. Also share with them that you are available to talk with them individually about any concerns they might have about themselves or a friend.

# Fishbowl Questions for Session 5

When others put me down, I....

One thing I really dislike about myself is....

I wish my parents knew....

I wear the kind of clothes I do because....

Things would be better in my family if only....

I secretly wish....

The best thing that could happen to my family....

I wish my teachers knew....

If I could change one thing about myself, I would....

One of the hardest things for me is....

# Session 6:
# The Mirror—How Others See Me

**Goal:** Group members will explore what image they present to others and discuss what desirable and undesirable characteristics others see in them.

**Materials:** Session 6: Fishbowl Questions

*Mirror Activity: How Others See Me* (page 63)

Markers/Crayons

Journal Entry and Journals

**Getting Started:** A group member will select a question from the fishbowl and respond to her question. There will be time for one or two brief comments from the group. The next group member will then select a question and respond. The process will repeat itself until each group member has been given the opportunity to respond to a question.

**Activity:** The Mirror Activity is designed to cover two sessions. For this session, group members will only be focusing on a handout copy of page 63. Give your group members copies of *Mirror Activity: How Others See Me* and instruct them to think about how others perceive them. It may be helpful to prompt them by having them think about how friends, parents, or siblings would describe them. Ask your group members to write phrases and/or draw pictures of how they think others perceive them on the *Mirror Activity: How Others See Me.*

Allow approximately 10 minutes for them to work on this individually. After they have completed the activity, encourage them to share their mirrors with the group. As they are sharing their perceptions of how they are viewed by others, ask for feedback from the others. ("Sue has just said that she thinks others see her as quiet and boring. Does anyone agree or disagree with this?") This is a powerful method to allow peers to provide constructive feedback about what they believe to be true. It also increases awareness of how one's behaviors and actions contribute to how one is perceived. This is an opportunity to develop connections among group members. ("Sue just said she thinks others see her as shy and unfriendly. I am wondering if anyone else feels this way?")

**Processing:**

Ask your group to discuss the following discussions:

**What is it like to feel that people see you the way they do?**

The purpose of this question is to encourage your group members to attach feelings to beliefs they have about how they are perceived. For example: Do they feel good about the way they are perceived? Does it make them angry to be perceived a certain way? Why do they feel this way?

**What is one thing others see in you that is not true?**

**How might they have gotten that impression?**

It is important to encourage your group members to begin to understand that not everything that others believe about them is accurate. For example, a group member may believe that others think she is dumb because she got a bad grade in one class. As the group leader, it is important to explore why these perceptions about a group member exist and to examine what individual behaviors contribute to this perception. For example, does the group member tell people she is dumb or does she "brag" publicly about bad grades? This question aims to empower group members to dispute perceptions others have about them that are not accurate. Additionally, by confronting behaviors that perpetuate the faulty perceptions, responsibility is placed on the group member to change these behaviors. In the situation above, the group member would be challenged to stop saying negative things about her academic performance.

**What is one thing others see in you that is true?**

**How did they know that about you?**

This question aims to help group members accurately identify what others see in them that they think is true. Again, the focus is on assisting them to link the concept that personal behavior/actions affect how others perceive them. The idea here is to reinforce the behaviors that they demonstrate which allow others to see their true self.

**Journal:**

Instruct your group members to respond to the following question in their journals:

How does it make you feel to receive feedback from other group members about yourself?

Do you agree/disagree with this feedback?

**Closing:**

Ask your group to share a sentence or two from their journal entries. It should be a quick thought or feeling statement that sums up her reaction to the group today. They should not read the entire journal entry—just share one small thought or feeling from it.

## Session 6: Fishbowl Questions

**When someone I like doesn't agree with me, I....**

**When I don't like someone who likes me, I....**

**One thing I like best about my personality is....**

**When someone I like doesn't like me, I....**

**The hardest thing about being a girl is....**

The hardest thing about being me is....

Something I wish people knew about me is....

I can't understand why people think I ....

One of the hardest things for me is....

People think I am....

## Mirror Activity: How Others See Me

# How Others See Me

## Session 7:
# The Mirror—How I See Myself

**Goal:** Group members will explore how the image they present to others differs from who they really are. Group members will then reflect and discuss honest perceptions of self-image.

**Materials:** Session 7: Fishbowl Questions

*Mirror Activity: How I See Myself* (page 68)

Markers/Crayons

Journal Entry and Journals

**Getting Started:** A group member will select a question from the fishbowl and respond to her question. There will be time for one or two brief comments from the group. The next group member will then select a question and respond. The process will repeat itself until each group member has been given the opportunity to respond to a question.

**Activity:** This session is a variation of the Mirror Activity in Session 6. For this session, group members will be given the *Mirror Activity: How Others See Me* and instructed to think about how they perceive themselves. It may be helpful to prompt the group members by having them think about what they see when they look in the mirror. Some questions that might be helpful to suggest would be:

What characteristic do you have?

What do you see that you like?

What do you see that you do not like?

Encourage your group to think beyond physical traits and to concentrate more on personality and emotions. Instruct them to write phrases and/or draw pictures of perceptions of self.

Allow approximately 10 minutes for them to work on this individually. After that, encourage them to share their mirrors with the group.

As individual group members share how they perceive themselves, solicit feedback from the others. For example, "Sue says that she sees herself as happy, friendly, and overweight. I am wondering what they other group members think about this?" As individuals hear how group members actually perceive them, they will be better equipped to begin to dispute negative perceptions about self.

**Processing:**   Ask your group to discuss the following questions:

> **What qualities do you see in yourself that you like?**

> **What qualities do you see in yourself that you do not like?**

The goal of these questions is to encourage statements about self that are positive and to allow the opportunity to practice saying positive things about self. When this question is asked, it is almost always easier for group members to discuss the characteristics they do not like. As the group leader, it is important to address this. (Why is it that it is so much easier to list negative things about ourselves than it is to list positive things about ourselves?)

> **How does your self-image affect the way you feel about yourself?**

The purpose of this question is to link thoughts about self to emotional state. For example, if a group member believes she is unattractive, how does this make her feel? It is important to insist that group members use words to describe feelings, not actions. In the example above, a common response would be, "I feel ugly and want to avoid talking to people," rather than, 'I feel sad and embarrassed."

> **How are your perceptions about yourself different/same as the way that others see you?**

Group members should reflect back on the previous session and compare/contrast how they view themselves and how others view them. They should be challenged to think about why it is that they view themselves differently than others view them. Encourage them to consider various possibilities:

> Do they only show a certain side of self to others?

> Is their behavior different around certain groups of people?

> Do they deliberately hide personality flaws?

**Journal:**   Instruct your group to reflect on the following question in their journals:

> What parts of yourself do you like?

**Closing:**   Ask your group members to share a sentence or two from their journal entries. It should be a quick thought or feeling statement that sums up her reaction to the group today. They should not read the entire journal entry—just share one small thought or feeling from it.

## Session 7: Fishbowl Questions

**When someone I like doesn't agree with me, I....**

**When I don't like someone who likes me, I....**

**One thing I like best about my personality is....**

**When someone I like doesn't like me, I....**

**The hardest thing about being a girl is....**

**The hardest thing about being me is.....**

**Something I wish people knew about me is.....**

**I can't understand why people think I .....**

**One of the hardest things for me is....**

**People think I am....**

## Mirror Activity: How I See Myself

# How I See Myself

Heather H. Barto and Sarah J. Salkeld

## Session 8:
# How Do the Television/Magazines Define Me? Messages from the Mass Media

**Goal:** Group members will explore beliefs about self in relation to how the mass media defines females. Group members will increase awareness of internalized messages about what girls should be and examine these beliefs via group discussion.

**Materials:** Session 8: Fishbowl Questions

Video Clip of Current Teen-Oriented Television Show

CD of Popular Song

Markers, Large paper and masking tape for the wall lists

Journal Entry and Journals

**Getting Started:** A group member will select a question from the fishbowl and respond to her question. There will be time for one or two brief comments from the group. The next group member will then select a question and respond. The process will repeat itself until each group member has been given the opportunity to respond to a question.

**Activity:** The activity will begin with a videotaped five-minute segment of a current television show that targets the adolescent age group. Examples of television shows may be *Dawson's Creek, Felicity,* or *Friends.*

After the group has viewed the segment, post paper on the wall and ask your group to brainstorm about how the television show portrays teen girls. All responses should be written on the paper.

At this point, facilitate a group discussion based on the processing questions that follow.

**Note:** Depending on time limitations, you may choose to repeat the activity/discussion format with the use of a current popular song.

**Processing:** Discuss the following questions.
(**Note:** There are only four questions. Having a limited number of questions is intentional on the part of the authors. Your group members will gain the most from this session by spending time processing the following questions in depth through open dialogue.)

> **What messages did the television show/song send about what girls should be?**

Encourage your students to reference the information previously posted on the wall about how girls are portrayed. For example, if one of the ideas posted was that the girls are always portrayed as well dressed and perfectly made-up, what message does this send girls about how they should look? The idea is to help them to identify some key beliefs that the mass media imposes on girls such as:

Girls should always be pretty and look fashionable.

Girls have to be thin to look good.

Girls should strive for perfection with physical beauty.

Negative qualities make girls less likable (i.e. bad skin, being overweight, not wearing the right clothing)

**Do you agree/disagree with these messages?**

This question simply allows group members to safely explore the idea that the messages sent by the media about what girls should be are not necessarily the same as their beliefs about what girls should be. The goal here is to allow for an open discussion about these messages. This will provide a nonthreatening opening into the next questions, which involve more self-analysis and personal reflection.

**How realistic are the messages that are portrayed?**

Your group members will probably be able to articulate that these messages are not very realistic. It is important to address the fact that although these messages are not always realistic, we still tend to believe them. At this point, you will want to address what is it about these messages that make us buy into them. It may be helpful to encourage your group members to think about why we buy certain clothing, hair products, and cosmetics. They could also reflect on what makes us interested in trying new products (shampoo, hair styling products, and make-up).

**Which of these messages do you believe to be true for you?**

Most students will have several beliefs that they reject, but they will usually have at least one belief about themself that is not realistic but they believe it to be true. For example, a group member may reject the idea that she has to be thin to be beautiful, but believe that she needs to have perfect skin to be likable. If your group members demonstrate difficulty identifying a belief that is true for them, you should provide an example of a belief that a female adult may have. An example of this would be: when a female develops wrinkles, she is no longer attractive.

The purpose of this question is to assist them in identifying specific beliefs that they subscribe to that impact their view of self. The important thing here is to encourage the girls to objectively look at self-definition without judging the belief. Suggested questions to help them process this further are:

What is it about this belief that makes you think it is true?

How does this belief impact how much you like yourself?

**Journal:**

Group members will revisit the belief about self that they identified as being true for them. Instruct them to spend five minutes reflecting/writing about the following:

Pretend that you no longer believe this belief about yourself. How would your life be different? How would things be better for you?

**Closing:**

Group members will be asked to share a sentence or two from their journal entries. It should be a quick thought or feeling statement that sums up her reaction to the group today. Group members should not read the entire journal entry-just share one small thought or feeling from it.

Heather H. Barto and Sarah J. Salkeld

## Session 8: Fishbowl Questions

**What if fat was beautiful?**

**What if being popular became unpopular?**

**One thing I think others see in me is....**

**I wish I could change....**

**What is one way boys are treated differently from girls by teachers?**

**What is one way boys are treated differently from girls by parents?**

**I wish my parents didn't expect me to....**

**I wish boys didn't expect girls to....**

**When I look at models in magazines, I feel....**

**When I look at models in magazines, I think....**

Heather H. Barto and Sarah J. Salkeld

# Session 9:
# How Do Boys Define Me?
# Messages from the Opposite Sex

**Goal:** Using a discussion format, group members will identify messages sent by the opposite sex in order to explore how these perceptions define self.

**Materials:** Session 9: Fishbowl Questions

*Name the Character* worksheet (page 77)

Markers, Large paper and masking tape for the wall

Journal Entry and Journals

**Getting Started:** A group member will select a question from the fishbowl and respond to her question. There will be time for one or two brief comments from the group. The next group member will then select a question and respond. The process will repeat itself until each group member has been given the opportunity to respond to a question. Make sure each group member gets a different question from the one they responded to in Session 8.

**Activity:** Group members will be placed into pairs and instructed to complete the *Name the Character* worksheet. Explain to them that they are going to write a television sitcom about a middle school. Instruct them to first review the list of characters with their partner and decide what to name each character.

Allow approximately five minutes for them to complete this task. Then, ask them to share with the group the names they selected for the cast of characters. Have blank copies of the worksheet available. As they are reading their list of names, record—next to each character—how many times they are given a male or a female name. After this has been completed, discuss the following:

What information did you use to decide if the character was male or female?

Why did you assume that some students were boys and others were girls?

Do we have certain expectations about what a girl/boy should be?

Where do these beliefs come from?

Ask your group to think of all the things that boys say about girls. What do boys say about how girls should be? Write all responses on the paper posted on the wall.

At this point, facilitate a group discussion based on the following processing questions.

**Processing:**

Discuss the following questions:

**How do boys want girls to look/act?**

Encourage them to reference the information previously posted on the wall about what boys want girls to be. For example, if one of the ideas posted was that boys want girls to be sexy, how does this define how a girl should look and act? (Short skirts, tight shirts, low necklines, etc.) The idea is to help girls identify specific physical traits/personality characteristics that they believe boys like. The goal is to build on the general statements that were posted on the wall to more clearly define these perceptions.

**Do you want to be this way?**

The purpose of this question is to help your group members challenge how others define what they should be. By challenging how others define self, they can then begin to develop definitions of self that are reflective of individual needs/wants. The goal of this discussion is not to bash everything that males say females should be, but to assist the girls in developing an identity that is not completely rooted in these belief systems. For example, can females wear jeans and still be considered sexy? If a girl wants to wear clothing that accentuates her figure, is this bad? What if a girl wants to wear sweat pants everyday?

**What would you want to change about the way boys view girls? How would this change how you feel about yourself?**

At this point, simply help them to clarify how the beliefs that boys have about girls make them feel. If all messages sent to us by boys made us feel good, we would not want to change anything about the way boys view girls. Thus, the beliefs that generate negative emotions (frustration, anger, and depression) need to be linked to negative feelings about self. (I am not likable; I am not pretty enough; I am not thin enough.) The important thing here is to encourage all group members to self reflect and to think about how these messages make them feel. Remind them frequently that there are no right or wrong answers.

**Journal:**

Group members will revisit what they would like to change about how boys view girls. Instruct them to spend five minutes reflecting/writing about the following:

Imagine that boys really did view girls the way you wanted them to. How would your life be different? How would this change how you feel about yourself?

**Closing:**

Group members will be asked to share a sentence or two from their journal entries. It should be a quick thought or feeling statement that sums up her reaction to the group today. Group members should not read the entire journal entry-just share one small thought or feeling from it.

## Session 9: Fishbowl Questions

**What if fat was beautiful?**

**What if being popular became unpopular?**

**One thing I think others see in me is....**

**I wish I could change....**

**What is one way boys are treated differently from girls by teachers?**

**What is one way boys are treated differently from girls by parents?**

**I wish my parents didn't expect me to....**

**I wish boys didn't expect girls to....**

**When I look at models in magazines, I feel....**

**When I look at models in magazines, I think....**

Heather H. Barto and Sarah J. Salkeld

# Name the Character

A student who is snobby towards other students. _____

A student who constantly gets suspended for fighting. _____

A student who is the class president and very smart. _____

A student who is not very smart, but very popular. _____

An honor roll student who works hard to do well in school. _____

The school principal. _____

A student who is very nice and respectful to the teachers. _____

A sixth grade music teacher in the school. _____

# Session 10:
# How Do My Parents Define Me?
# Examining Parental Messages

**Goal:**

Group members will explore beliefs about self in relation to parental expectations.

Group members will identify internalized messages and increase awareness of how parental messages have impacted the definition of self.

**Materials:**

Session 10: Fishbowl Questions

*A World of Wishes* worksheet (page 82)

Markers, Large paper and masking tape for the wall

Journal Entry and Journals

**Getting Started:**

A group member will select a question from the fishbowl and respond to her question. There will be time for one or two brief comments from the group. The next group member will then select a question and respond. The process will repeat itself until each group member has been given the opportunity to respond to a question. Again make sure that each group member gets a different question from those she answered in the two previous sessions.

**Activity:**

Ask your group members to think of all the things that their parents say about how girls should behave. How do their parents want them to act? How do they want them to dress? Write all responses on paper posted on the wall.

Then instruct them to complete *A World of Wishes* worksheet. Explain to the group members that they should identify three expectations their parents have for them about how they should be. After each expectation, have them write down how they wish this expectation would be different. It may be helpful to provide one example for them based upon one of the responses posted on the wall.

Allow approximately ten minutes for the group to complete this. Ask them to share at least one of the expectations/wishes with the group. Discuss the following with your group:

**How do you feel about the way your parents want you to be?**

Encourage your group members to evaluate how these beliefs make them feel. Often students will respond with action words rather than feeling words, such as: "I feel like fighting or I want to run away." It is much easier to use action words, but it is important to assist them in identifying the underlying emotions they feel in response to what others say they should be.

At this point, facilitate a group discussion based on the following processing questions.

Heather H. Barto and Sarah J. Salkeld

**Processing:**   Discuss the following questions:

> **How realistic are the beliefs your parents have about how girls should be?**

The group members undoubtedly will have several examples of beliefs their parents have that they feel are unrealistic about how girls should be. The goal here is to help them sort out the beliefs that they have internalized from parental messages and to begin to explore the beliefs they do not agree with. It is not necessary to place judgment on the parental beliefs, rather, it is important to allow space for them to safely begin to separate their beliefs about self from their parents' beliefs about self. Individuating self from parents is an important developmental stage; however, adolescents often choose to challenge parental beliefs in the heat of an argument, rather than through reflective thought.

> **We have talked during the last three sessions about how the television, boys, and our parents define how girls are supposed to be. How do you know what to believe about yourself? How do you define yourself? What do you want to be about?**

The purpose of these questions is to assist your group members in reflecting on the past three sessions. It may be helpful to briefly review what was discussed in each of these sessions. They need to be encouraged to think about what these sessions have taught them about themselves. Have the discussions led to more/less self acceptance? Have they learned anything about themselves that they are surprised by? If they had to write a description of themselves, what would it say? The idea is to show the group members the process of moving towards a more positive view of self. By this point in the group, they should be able to identify how feelings about self are impacted by how others perceive them, (i.e., parents, boys, peers, media).

**Journal:**   Ask the group to revisit the last question addressed in the group discussion. How do you want to define yourself?

Pretend you are moving out of state to live with your grandmother. You will be starting off the school year in a new school in your grandmother's town. As you prepare for the first day of school, think about the following. How will you act on the first day of school? How will you dress? What will you do to allow other students to know what you are all about? Describe yourself as you want to be perceived.

**Closing:**   Ask them to share a sentence or two from their journal entries. It should be a quick thought or feeling statement that sums up her reaction to the group today. They should not read the entire journal entry—just share one small thought or feeling from it.

## Session 10: Fishbowl Questions

**What if fat was beautiful?**

**What if being popular became unpopular?**

**One thing I think other see in me is....**

**I wish I could change....**

**What is one way boys are treated differently from girls by teachers?**

**What is one way boys are treated differently from girls by parents?**

**I wish my parents didn't expect me to....**

**I wish boys didn't expect girls to....**

**When I look at models in magazines, I feel....**

**When I look at models in magazines, I think....**

# A World of Wishes

## My parents expect...

1 _____

_____

2 _____

_____

3 _____

_____

## If I could change these expectations, I wish...

1 _____

_____

2 _____

_____

3 _____

_____

Heather H. Barto and Sarah J. Salkeld

# Session 11:
# Group Collage—"The Real Female"

**Goal:** Group members will explore the concepts of self-esteem body image in order to show increased awareness of distorted perceptions and demonstrate new knowledge of more accurate perceptions by creating a collage representing the "real female."

**Materials:** Session 11: Fishbowl Questions

Glue

Scissors

Magazines

Journal Entry and Journals

**Getting Started:** A group member will select a question from the fishbowl and respond to her question. There will be time for one or two brief comments from the group. The next group member will then select a question and respond. The process will repeat itself until each group member has been given the opportunity to respond to a question.

**Note:** For this set of question strips, each one says the same thing: Ask someone in the group a question about something you would like to know about her—the more difficult the better.

**Activity:** Group members will work individually to create a collage depicting a "real female." They will most likely not need to be encouraged to talk and get to know each other through casual conversation. It is interesting to observe how the dynamics of the group have changed since the first collage. If things are going well, you should feel as if you are not even needed at this point. However, remember if you had not done a good job as the group's leader, things would not be going this well now. It is also important to remember you are still needed to help the group stay focused and work hard.

**Processing:** This collage activity will be fully processed in the next session. The purpose of this session is to allow the group members time to work on their collages while learning more about each other and sharing about themselves. It should be interesting for you to observe the interactions between them. You may even want to reflect some of your observations back to the group. For example, you might say something like:

> It seems as though you have a much easier time talking now than you did when we worked on the first collage. What do you think is different now?

**Journal:** Take the last few minutes of the session to have them respond in their journals to the following writing prompt:

> Describe the "real female."

**Closing:** Ask your group to share a sentence or two from their journal entries. It should be a quick thought or feeling statement that sums up her reaction to the group today. Group members should not read the entire journal entry— just share one small thought or feeling from it.

## Session 11: Fishbowl Questions

**Ask someone in the group a question about something you would like to know about her—the more difficult the better.**

**Ask someone in the group a question about something you would like to know about her—the more difficult the better.**

**Ask someone in the group a question about something you would like to know about her—the more difficult the better.**

**Ask someone in the group a question about something you would like to know about her—the more difficult the better.**

**Ask someone in the group a question about something you would like to know about her—the more difficult the better.**

Heather H. Barto and Sarah J. Salkeld

**Ask someone in the group a question about something you would like to know about her—the more difficult the better.**

**Ask someone in the group a question about something you would like to know about her—the more difficult the better.**

**Ask someone in the group a question about something you would like to know about her—the more difficult the better.**

**Ask someone in the group a question about something you would like to know about her—the more difficult the better.**

**Ask someone in the group a question about something you would like to know about her—the more difficult the better.**

# Session 12:
# Group Closure

**Goal:**

Group members will explore the concept of self-esteem in order to increase awareness of distorted perceptions by creating a collage representing the "real female."

Group members will learn more about other group members in order to increase group cohesion by engaging in casual conversation guided by the group leader.

**Materials:**

Question Fishbowl: *Strength Bombardment Sheets* (see page 88)

Journal Entry and Journal

All materials collected from group members during the course of the group, (i.e., collages, journal, handouts, mirror activity)

*Group Evaluation* (see page 89)

**Getting Started:**

Each group member will select a *Strength Bombardment Sheet* from the fishbowl. Each student should take a second to look at the blank sheet and write her name at the top of the sheet. Then the group passes the sheets to the left and each person writes something that she likes or admires about the person whose name is at the top of the sheet. The group will continue passing at your cues until they have circulated through the entire group. The group members will then be given a minute to read their sheet silently.

**Note:** You may choose to wait until the end of the session to do this activity.

**Activity:**

Group members will compare the collages that they have made depicting the "perfect female" and depicting a "real female." They should be encouraged to talk about what they have learned by participating in the group. (See Processing Section.)

**Processing:**

This is the last group session and should provide the group with some closure. It is important to allow every member ample time to share what she has learned and what she has felt by participating in the group. It is often best to throw out questions to the group and allow them to discuss them in an open format. However, make sure each person has time to speak. Possible questions to use are:

- What have you learned from being in this group?
- What new ideas have you thought about since you started participating in this group?
- What feelings have these activities and discussions given you?
- How are you going to put what you have learned into action?

Heather H. Barto and Sarah J. Salkeld

**Journal:**

Take the last few minutes of the group to have them respond in their journals to the following writing prompt:

What was the most important part of this group for you?

**Closing:**

Ask your group members to share one final thought from their group experience. They should be thoughts or feeling statements that sum up their reactions to the group experience. Have your group members complete the *Group Evaluation*. Make sure that you give them all of the items that you have collected from them during the course of the group. Encourage them to look at these items periodically over the next few months to remind them of what they learned.

## Strength Bombardment Sheet

# What I like about _____

Heather H. Barto and Sarah J. Salkeld

# Group Evaluation

|  | Agree |  | Neutral |  | Disagree |
|---|---|---|---|---|---|
| I liked group. | 1 | 2 | 3 | 4 | 5 |
| I felt comfortable in the group. | 1 | 2 | 3 | 4 | 5 |
| I shared things with the group. | 1 | 2 | 3 | 4 | 5 |
| I felt supported by the leader. | 1 | 2 | 3 | 4 | 5 |
| I learned more about myself. | 1 | 2 | 3 | 4 | 5 |
| I learned more about my family. | 1 | 2 | 3 | 4 | 5 |
| I learned about other group members. | 1 | 2 | 3 | 4 | 5 |

I learned _____

_____

_____

The most helpful part of group was _____

_____

_____

The group could have been improved by _____

_____

_____

I thought the leader was _____

_____

A topic I wish we would have talked about was _____

_____

Other suggestions or comments _____

_____

_____

Heather H. Barto and Sarah J. Salkeld

# Chapter 5

# Resources

# Suggestions for Counselors

## Books

American Association of University Women (1992). *Shortchanging girls, shortchanging America.* Washington DC: AAUW Educational Foundation and National Education Association.

> This report provides research and statistics about how girls are often at a disadvantage in the classroom. The research offers information about how girls are perceived differently from boys in the educational setting.

Berg, F.M. (1997). *Afraid to eat: Children and teens in weight crisis.* Hettinger, ND: Healthy Weight Journal.

> This book was written by a nutritionist who challenges America's obsession with weight. In this book, the author discusses why diets don't work and chronicles the harm done by the quest for thinness.

Costin, C. (1999). *The Eating disorders sourcebook: A comprehensive guide to the causes, treatment, and prevention of eating disorders.* Los Angeles, CA: Lowell House.

> This book was written by a recovering anorexic and eating disorders specialist. It provides a professional viewpoint of the topic of eating disorders and examines individual and family dynamics involved with eating disorders.

Gilligan, C. (1990). *Making connections: The relational worlds of adolescent girls at Emma Willard School.* Cambridge, MA: Harvard University Press.

Kolodny, N. (1998). *When food's a foe: How to confront and conquer your eating disorder.* Boston, MA: Little Brown.

> This book discusses recent research on the topic of eating disorders and offers information on support resources.

Pipher, M. (1994). *Reviving Opheila: Saving the selves of adolescent girls.* New York, NY: G.P. Putnam's Sons.

> This book provides insight into the world of an adolescent girl as witnessed through a psychologist working with this population. It combines recent research with case histories to portray the realities of being an adolescent female in today's culture.

Siegel, M.. (1997). *Surviving an eating disorder: Strategies for family and friends.* New York, NY: Harper Perennial.

> This book explores the serious dangers of eating disorders and offers effective strategies for working with individuals suffering from eating disorders. The book provides practical solutions and support for friends and families of those with eating disorders.

Heather H. Barto and Sarah J. Salkeld

# Suggested Resources for Adolescent Girls

## Books

Bolden, T. (1998). *33 things every girl should know: Stories, songs, poems, and smart talk by 33 extraordinary women.* New York, NY: Crown.

> This book is offers advice and insights for adolescent girls through a collection of short stories, interviews, essays and poems.

Bode, J. (1997). *Food fight: A guide to eating disorders for preteens and their parents.* New York, NY: Simon and Schuster Books for Young Readers.

> This book is written for parents and adolescents. It provides suggestions and self-help information about gaining control over eating habits.

Davis, B. (1999). *What's real, what's ideal.* New York, NY: Rosen Publishing Group.

> This book explores the relationship between perceptions of body image and overall psychological health. Through the use of short stories this book discusses the causes of negative body image.

Gadeberg, J. (1997). *Brave new girls: Creative ideas to help girls be confident, healthy, and happy.* Minneapolis, MN: Fairview Press.

> This book is a practical guide to helping adolescents handle the problems of growing up. Topics include family relationships, body image and sexual harassment.

Gottlieb, L. (2000). *Stick figure: A diary of my former self.* New York, NY: Berkley Books.

> This is a fictional account of an individual with an eating disorder. It chronicles the struggle an adolescent girl encounters as she starves herself in an attempt to create the perfect figure.

Hornbacher, M. (1999). *Wasted: A memoir of anorexia and bulimia.* New York, NY: Haper Collins Publishing.

> This book is written by a 23-year-old recovering anorexic. It portrays her downward spiral to extreme thinness.

Pohlman, S. (1998). *A girl's guide to life: The complete instructions.* New York, NY: Penguin Books.

> This book was written by adolescents for adolescents. It offers a compilation of advice, helpful hints and expert opinions from adolescents across the country.

Shandler, S. (1999). *Ophelia speaks: Adolescent girls write about their search for self.* New York, NY: Harper Perennial.

> This book offers writings from teenage girls on subjects ranging from body image to boys, school to sex, parents to politics. This book provides insightful thoughts for adolescents as well as an opportunity for educators to better understand the world of a teenage girl.

Weston, C. (1998). *For girls only: Wise words, good advice.* New York, NY: Avon Books.

> This book offers adolescent girls wise words in the form of affirmations, insights and advice. Topics include friendship, family, school and self.

## Magazines

"Eating Disorders: The Toll There are Taking on Teens." *Teen Magazine.* February, 1999.

> This magazine article provides factual information and stories about individuals confronting eating disorders.

"Out of Control." *People Magazine.* February 12, 1999.

> This magazine article chronicles the difficulties recovering anorexics and bulimics face as they struggle to overcome their eating disorders.

## Videos

(All videos are available through www.caringonline.com)

*The Best Little Girl in the World*

> This video is a fictional portrayal of an adolescent girl with anorexia. It explores the relationship between family dynamics and the development of eating disorders.

*Cathy Rigby on Eating Disorders*

> Cathy Rigby, a former bulimic, narrates this educational program which focuses on the process of recovery.

*Trouble in Mind: Eating Disorders*

> This video provides educational information on the topic of eating disorders.

Heather H. Barto and Sarah J. Salkeld